MW01532248

To Showing Myself More Love,

****

Le-Aisha Lenae Meyers

Le-Aisha Lenae Meyers

1

To Showing Myself More Love,

♡

it's never too late.

THANKS

to mom and dad for creating me and always being proud of it. *to* my mom, you're a perfect example of a true friend, my best friend. you're my motivation *to* go harder, my motivation *to* never give up. thanks for holding it down even when you struggled *to* hold yourself up. you'll always be my most dearest possession. *to* my dad, I've been blessed with your cool, calm, and collected nature, you'll always have a special place in my heart, you were the first person to love me for me, so i'll always be me around you, thanks for the validation. and not just the proof that says i'm beautiful but the proof that says i am *everything*. to kayla, *to* my siblings this is ultimately for you, i'll forever be your keeper, i only hope that you'll be better than me, never limit yourself and never forget to show yourself love. *to* anyone i've ever crossed paths with and shared laughs with, *to* anyone i've ever said i love you to, and *to* anyone who has ever said they love me, thank you.

Authors Note:

Sometimes I wish I could be more open with people
about myself.
But I'm slowly breaking out of sheltering my being
because it's not always about protecting my story it's
about helping others realize that everyone has a story
they need to embrace.
It's not that I care about what people think it's just
that I'm not a victim and I don't ever want to be
perceived as that.
There were times when I felt like the victim and there
were times in the past where I hurt someone else but
I am not a victim;
Not today or tomorrow or ever again. I embrace my
story because everything I learned and everything
I've seen and felt has shaped me to be the person I am
today.
And I love the person I am today.
I love the person I was yesterday and way back then
when I thought I loved too much.
Or when I dwelled on how I didn't receive enough
love or when I wasn't aware that I wasn't receiving
enough love
I don't ever want to feel like I love too much again
because I was put on this earth to love and to be
loved.
I will always love people I'm close to more than they
love me even when I don't show it.

I see beauty in everyone and everything and I know
that's one of the things that make my life so damn
difficult sometimes.
But I will never sacrifice my heart, this heart is gold.
It's genuine and it wishes people well.
It's forgiving, it keeps my mind filled with positive
thoughts even after I've felt pain.
My heart feeds my brain. So much it makes it seem
like I don't care about nothing because I care about
everything.
I care about myself now more than anything. So even
when I still love you I understand when I can't give
you my love anymore.
It's different these days, these days I can miss you
and you'll never know because I'm learning how to
let go.
I'm just out here setting shit free, that's what my
heart has been up to.
I don't believe in holding on to anyone that wants to
roam I don't believe in holding on to anyone that
can't see that I'm worth a sacrifice,
I don't believe in holding on to anyone who feels they
are better off without me.
See the thing with my heart is I know when I'm the
best thing for you
Even before you know I'm the best thing for you.

I don't commit to something or someone I won't give
my best to.
Everyone can't feel that.
I can't love everyone the same way.
But when I love you too much, I just know and it's
funny because you'll just know too.
And you might run away from it because I'm
someone that you can spend forever with but you're
not ready for forever right now.
And you see my heart gets that shit.
Its open and its understanding but it feeds my mind
to always love me at the end of the day.
To always remember that you have the best love for
you
That the heart that you want to share with others
you're still blessed to have it inside of you.
These days are different. I probably won't be back
after I let go these days, I just feel like I owe myself
someone who loves me *too* much.
And one day I'm going to be ready for it and I'm going
to get that,
And I'm going to feel that
And I can't feel that looking back or treating myself as
some sort of victim
For loving after being let down so many times
Not when I'm a winner.

To Showing Myself More Love,

half-grown.

To Showing Myself More Love,

Who was I when you approached me and courted me and told em all I belonged to you when they tried me? what did your eyes see? Because I saw everything that made me believe that I'd have a chance at my own fairytale. Couldn't let you have it so soon, but I went home and couldn't get you out of my room out of my mind I was going out of my mind, wanted to know how being in your possession would feel, called my best friend it was a big a deal, we talked for hours she said I should try it, so I found my way to you...

turns out i was finding my way to me.

Pride.

I always looked at you and felt safe
You didn't always have it together
You were the first one to call me beautiful, and smart,
and lay big wet kisses on my cheeks that I hated but
loved at the same time. I made you proud.
You spoke highly of me to the point where I would be
embarrassed by all of the attention.
You were happy to have me as your daughter, first
born, the splitting image of you but the pretty version
because of the gentleness of my mom.
I valued me, I felt like anyone, whoever they were
would have to be as happy, as boastful and as prideful
as you were to have me, to claim me.
You weren't always around though.
Months almost years without speaking to you or
seeing you, luckily the memories of you always
resonated, always reminded me of who I am, always
kept my self-esteem high enough,

I always let you back in because you were my dad
Because even though I resented you for not being
there, when you were there you was *there*. Present.
Out of anyone in the world I believed you when you
said you were proud of me, I believed you when you
said you were proud of me and would die for me. You
looked at me and smiled a big smile.
I got my big smile from you
You would come and go as if we didn't matter, you
had a new family and they got to see you all the time.
But you never checked in.
I guess you knew my mom was a good woman and
your kids were in good hands. We were used to it.
I guess you knew your daughter was smart, strong
and could always hold her own.

I guess you knew my little sister had two great
women to look up to, to keep her pure even though
she would grow to resent you too but love you all in
one breath

I learned how to hold it down, we held it down, as
women who never applied pressure to men because
they were never obligated to stay.
I learned how to let people like you come in and out
of my life just as long as I knew they took pride in
claiming someone like me.
You see I put myself through a lot of heartbreak not
understanding that I didn't need any validation
For what I already knew.
I always let him come back because he loved me like
you did, a lot. Boastfully, proudly, but with distance,
not enough to stay, not enough to watch me grow day
by day only to see the finished product every season.
He'll come back when the flowers bloomed in spring,
after my skin browned, when pumpkins bring family
together, and when the snow cleared. He knew I'd be
good regardless. I appreciated the assurance but still
yearned for the love.

I understand him like I understood you.
Everyone has their own life to live,
I get it, and no one is entitled to stick with me not
even you.
So who am I to make anyone stay, who am I to
demand the presence of anyone who claims they love
me.

13

16.

Summer nights in Harlem
Whipping down Lenox Avenue, in the hoop-tie
God got us covered knowing the day was going to
come when we would be in a foreign.
Sweet love,
Always knew we were more than what we saw
More than the blue hoop-tie
More than the recycled girls and boys
More than the triggers that took our high school
friends
We were bigger than Lenox Ave
Our minds expanded past 8th Avenue
Past Dyckman
Never felt like I needed someone else
Just you.
I knew we would have everything we wanted one day
And I wanted you to be the one to give it to me
Big thoughts, thinking small always made us
uncomfortable
You got me.
I got you.

eight-teen.

Always told me God got us
While we ate in the car
And shared our drinks cause even if I got my own
You would drink it anyway
And I'd clown you and call you thirsty
And then beg you to drive me downtown to work
And you always did
See we never wanted to be apart
We'd text right after you pulled off,
After kissing goodbye and asking for one more which
turned into five more
Kisses.
My way of letting you know
I ain't want to let you go not ever
Butta soft
Always loved you in your buttas even with your butta
soft.
If it's one thing we did,
We did us.
Dressed, stayed down
Always showed respect
Power couple before we even
Got the power.
Young and in love

we used to do it everywhere
remember we almost got caught
I swear,
Couldn't nobody tell you nothing about me
There was a time where
I could do no wrong,
I was your angel
Remember that year you lost your grandma and you
found me
And you always said she would have loved me,
And that's probably why you loved me.
That always made me feel like
God got us.

The innocence
The pure bliss, toast to believing true love exist
To feeling like I'm in a fairytale
I found the one and I am the one.

seize

I've seen you cheat on my dearest and leave my dearest for that fun experience. I've seen fourteen years and two kids go down the drain but I've seen the friendship maintained. I love like my dearest, a forgiving lover, an unconditional friend even when the conditions never benefit you in the end. I've heard you say she's still your best friend even though you've made a wife out of the next woman. What is love? I've tried to understand from eight years old and year eight when we let go, curious to know what does it all even mean. I've feared me going through what my dearest has, so i've mastered the act of holding on and letting go *simultaneously* with hopes he'll experience but wont go astray for too long. I've sighed with relief every time we'd fall in love again, but the list of outsiders continued to grow along side my insecurities. I've come to know every girl that could have potentially taken my love, I've learned something from every girl, there's a little piece of every girl in me. My dearest hasn't found a notable love again, and probably never have and that made me weary. I didn't want to be my dearest and just having someone who loved me meant the most, so I tried to control my first love being my last, I couldn't stop believing in forever.

half-grown

Half figured out, thought I knew it all. Half-grown but
quite ready for more, ready for more with the one I
adored. Remember that night I cried on your lap. And
you whispered I told you so.
Two years ago you said I was too young to be so
serious, too young to have a boyfriend, but I wasn't
too young to feel. I couldn't stop feeling. In fact, he felt
the same. Half grown too young to know I didn't have
it all figured out, I figured out self-respect didn't
mean I loved myself, cause I was still surprised
someone loved me. Still surprised someone choose
me. I've never been chosen. I didn't think I was good
enough until I found someone who thought I was
good enough. That mattered the most to me. I was
attached to a fairytale and dove right in. I climbed on
your lap like a baby and you cradled me, I cried
hysterically for the first time on you. Opened up new
doors with you. That moment you became my best
friend, the person who would always carry me from
birth to now, half-grown, in my mamas' lap letting the
world have it. When mama knows best starts making
sense, I told myself I'd never let you see me cry again,
but we've cried again. I couldn't stop my tears I

couldn't hide my wounds, first heartbreaks really
show you who you are. How much I didn't know love,
I didn't know me. Me was us. Took me a while to get
my head straight, begged and blamed myself for not
knowing better, for failing at love, the one person
who had me didn't need me how I needed them.
While I was drowning they were so unbothered still
so very much alive who prepared them for this?

appeal

I walk outside to different stares and different
remarks that would have me confused a while back
I was already inside trying to bring myself outside
Fighting with myself over what feels comfortable
What would bring less attention, what made my
curves look too appealing,
I didn't want to look too appealing.
I got dressed and undressed about 5 times with the
thoughts of how the outside world would react
My dress, my plain black dress was too form fitted, it
made my hips accentuate and made my ass stand out
I didn't want to walk down the street with a high
chance of being stalked or a high chance of hearing
damn she has a fat ass.
Yes behold this fat ass that you cannot touch
And a phat pussy that you don't have access too,

To Showing Myself More Love,

undeniably I've had it up to here with the annoyance of making women feel uncomfortable as they walk down the street minding their business with the weight of the world on their shoulders, after they've just forced themselves out the house hoping they have conformed to the beauty standards of today. Seems as if I have some of the beauty standards of today, I wish my inside capabilities and skills were shown on the outside,
Why can't I hear damn she's articulate or damn she put her outfit together so nice instead.
Can I feel like art instead of a sex object that you would love to toss up and down.

I've been tossed up and down enough.

you have the body of a model
you should model
and you have the body of a forty-five year-old man

I'm eleven.

essentially

I'll leave and I'll come back again, forever and ever for you, it feels like I'll feel you forever for me. I'll try to love myself a little more every time I leave, pep talk myself to walk away give you another two weeks to find your way, and in the midst of it try to tell myself I'm doing the right thing, essentially. I never really leave for real, but I'll stay away a little longer every time, still feel you every time, try to find my pride every time, and then come back because you're mine, essentially. You belong to me, no one else gets to claim you out loud, you said you loved me, that matters right? I know you only really expect forever from me, essentially.

Maybe.

I've laid next to you wondering if you even really like
me.
If I was even enough, if I had to be someone else.
Maybe I had to change my hair or change how I
dressed.
Maybe I had to take a little bit from every one of your
lies so that you could have your perfect lie in one. I've
tarnished while lying next to a body that doesn't
appreciate the smoothness of my skin or
the presence of me after a long day. How I'd crave
your smile and words from your long day to rock me
to sleep. I've always felt at home with a body that had
doubts that I was the one. A body that loved me to
death but always felt the need to let me go, always
felt the need to remind me that this is all wrong.

How I feel is not that important to the big idea, the
idea that first loves can never be your last. First loves
are practice. You cannot find your prince before you
fall for the frogs.
We cannot be, this is too good to be.
A body that pushed me away time after time when
we would get too close.
We were always so close to serenity. A body that
loved the way I kissed the skin under its eyes to make
it relax because it knew no one ever thought to love
that part of them.
I've examined every part of you just in case you
didn't know how beautiful you were I could then
recite the millions of ways you were worthy. From
the back of your knees up and around, full circle
I thanked God for you.

Recognize:

"to identify as something or someone previously
seen. To perceive as existing or true. To acknowledge
or treat as valid. To show appreciation of. "

I recognize
I've been here before
Feels like home, feels like Saturday morning
I love Sunday afternoons
Waking up cooking breakfast
Got babe in the room
Back in tune back to doing what we do
I've been here before
Now it feels like my backs against the wall
Sliding down the wall, tears coming down my face
Got me falling on the floor
I'm always falling on the floor
I recognize this shit I swear I've been here before
This is going to be one of those nights that carry over
into it being one of those mornings
Where I wake up looking like last night
Looking like I had a bad night
Puffy eyes from crying
I'm tired of crying when I know I'm just mad at
myself
I recognize all this hurt
You can't recognize that you dragged me through the

dirt
Go ahead tell me that you love me more

Then go lay with someone else
Sick of picturing you giving yourself to someone else
I feel like you're trying to make me used to it
I could never get used to it
I recognize the lust
But then I recognize the love
Probably why I'm falling apart
You know you are my heart
But I recognize the dark and I recognize the lies and
the uncertainty in your eyes
But I try to change my mind
Hoping for better every time
Time I recognize myself and put back on my winners
belt
Can't keep recognizing pain not when it was love that
brought me here
I have to keep it moving
So you can recognize yourself and get to know this
loss
Because everything you did
will make you better for *someone else.*

To Showing Myself More Love,

If only we could just get it right.

New Feel.

Never thought it would come to this.
Three years ago we kissed and the kiss wasn't all that
great.
But it was exciting. I never had someone try to
swallow me whole.
You were so aggressive, so passionate when you seen
me that day.
The first day.
You wasted no time to show me how much you
adored me.
How soon of you to show how you feel
I loved that you never tried to hide the way I brung
you out of your element.
We had just met but it was like you knew what you
wanted.
So I gave you what you wanted.
I felt sexy,
I felt like a woman.
You referred to me as a woman.
So I gave it up like a woman
Who knew what she wanted even though she didn't
know what she wanted.
I was grown.
I didn't care.

"Live a little because your man seems to live a lot, this
is your time."
It was my body, my body
Wanted to feel every inch of you,
It had only been four days but we were comfortable
I wanted to see what I was missing.
Because just last week I still felt like I was *half-grown.*
I wanted to see if I would feel it in my stomach.
Or if it would knock on my heart and make me fall in
love.
I wanted to see what I was missing, because the one
who had my heart was living.
I wanted to see if it would confuse me
Like if every inch stood for the number of years I
would be stuck on you.
Like if the width would have me open.
You were my sweet experience
You let me know how I wanted to feel
During a time where I didn't feel like I was enough
During a time where I had to be reminded who the
hell I was
Like how I loved having someone who would sweat
me
Because I was always the one to pour myself on to
them
I was always the one blatantly showing love
It felt good for the moments

And three months later it feels good for the moments
But I know you know this ain't it
I know you know that
No matter how much of a woman you made me feel
You couldn't reach my heart and tap it hard enough
To change where I laid my head at night.

I always went back to him and you always came back
to me
Some things I wish I could take from you
To put it in him but of all things
I just wanted him to make me feel like a woman
Not you, not the guy who told me I was beautiful on
the train this morning,
Not the guy who couldn't stop staring at me
Just him.
We could never be what you wanted it to be and yet
you still care
You still like me for me, friend-zoned.
You let me know you rock with me for who I am
As you patiently wait for the next time
Our bare skin creates wetness.
Till the next time I show you how much I've grown.
I know you still daydream to the sounds of my
moaning
Three years ago
Thanks for making me feel like a woman.

switch.

You had fell for me too, time and time again
reasons why I could never stop being a fool for you,
we've reversed roles and you stayed through guilt,
but something tells me it was through love,
something always tells me it's love, when the hurt is
never physical or blatant disrespect. I finally made
you cry and something told you you owed me more
than high hopes and butterflies from your presence,
it made you feel dead inside when the one thing you
knew, gave away part of you.

We Know.

Hated how
How your words would talk a good one
But your actions would let me down
You love me
I know.
I know
It's just that, I want this
I don't know if you want this
It feels like you don't know if you want this
Cold feet, no wedding though
Cause it probably really won't be no wedding
But you love me to death
I know
Would take a bullet for me
I know
Go to jail for me
I know
I feel that
I feel that you love me
I feel it all
But I question if you want this
Let me know
Put yourself first

I want you to
I want you to know that
I get it
I get it all

Life happens
But I still feel like
I can call you
I know I can call on you
I know you would come
I know you would drop everything
And pick me up if someone knocks me down
I feel that
You're my best friend
Through distance, through time,
Through pain, through love
I know that
Just not the best lover
You can't be that
I get it
Not right now
Life happens.

I thought we promised to always
Make it through whatever I just really hope that
You're not gone forever.

Where there's so much life to see
how do I know you're the one for me, if I stayed and
committed to the woman you are, what would be
your experiences outside of me, outside of us.
Would you be okay with just me, no regrets, just me
stories to share of just me. I just want you to find you
without me.

Where there's so much life to see I'd like to think
everything would be just a bit more beautiful with you
beside me. I am us I like being about us.

you know me.

*How fulfilling is it to know that there can be no in
between,
we can only be one or nothing,
everything and not just something.
to those days where we've shouted in anger and in
self-righteousness, to those days we hold in contempt,
part of the reasons why this is what it is, we've only
wanted to understand ourselves, and the chemistry
that lived in our heads,
formulated I love you's, but I gotta do this for me's
I get the hurt one can feel from hurting the other now,
I understand the agony, the tear that dropped knowing
this would be the last time, and hating the timing of it
all. On this journey of finding out who we are
there's this pain, this knot in your throat that you can't
swallow when you've gotta let go
As you go about your days thinking about the one who
got away, hoping
God is listening.*

To Showing Myself More Love,

Life forced us to let go
I don't know who told life that was what we wanted
But life got the word
Somebody wasn't being honest
Somebody couldn't keep their promises.

resentment.

What is love from another with too much pride to pour out their love to you? What is love from a another who isn't patient enough to see you grow? What is love from a someone who can do no wrong, who doesn't see how their wrongs, turned you cold. I've had this thing from a man, it was always gentle pain, always kept me wondering, never kept me safe, kept me coming back and I changed every time I came, to not enough still, to this and to that, until I changed so much that I never came back.

There's pain when I can't recite how beautiful our love was, I'd like to. At times I can't quite remember more good than bad, but I know there was more good than bad... we cried hard the first time we were separated and had to live in separate cities, I think there's beauty in that. In being so in love you're scared distance would change that. I would really like to remember the moments, the kind words we exchanged, the times you only trusted me, I think that hurts more, the loss of memory when you try to let the pain go. I'd like to remember how two imperfect human beings so naive in love and life clung to one another, times you protected my sensitive nature, my innocence, you led I followed. There's pain in knowing the potential of it all, and never quite getting there.

Why I could never go back

I think I went back too many times
I think you came back too many times
How many times does it take for you to see that what
you have here
Is all you need
It's gotten to the point where I could never go back
This time I love me too much
Like legit,
I love me better than anyone ever has,
well at least *I'm trying to*
I finally realized
My worth
And I don't know if you're aware that
On this earth there is only one me
I don't think you ever appreciated how you were
enough
And I mean you
That side I've only seen, the stories you've only told
me.
I don't think you've felt my absence enough
I think somewhere in your brain you think this is a
forever thing

And you can pick me up and put me down, fall back
on me.
Love me then tell me I'm doing everything wrong
Times when I would think our love was sweet
I used to think every day was a sunny day as long as I
woke up next to you
Because I knew how to put shit behind us.
I put too much behind us
To make it work, for it to not work.
You made me feel like I was asking for too much
any time I wanted answers,
any time I wanted to build a life with the love of my
life
I knew how to hide the hurt because our bond was
more important to me
Than me.
You told me I was in love with the idea of love.
When you know I've only ever really loved you.
When you know it's hard for me to even like someone
new.
As if I don't love being alone
As if I wasn't happily alone before I met you.
When I just wanted to make plans with you
You made me question if I was really in love with you
Because you wasn't sure if you were in love with me.
You crossed the line.
Not once, not twice, I can count
Three four five times, I let things slide that I would
never let slide again
I feel resentment every night at about 3AM

Because I know I should have let you go
Sooner.
Four years ago would have sufficed.
God gave me signs and I put you before God,
I believed God didn't put us together to not be
together
So we were gonna be together.
I thought maybe if we get all this bullshit out the way
while we were young
Then we'll be good to go by 23.
But here I am at 24
and you left me.
Again.
So if he doesn't know by now he never will
You made me wish I let go
two thousand tears ago.
You made me hurt you back.
I never wanted to hurt you back
You made me realize I was being naïve
When I trusted you.
I trusted your heart
I trusted your love, and your words
But I could never go back.
My love for me won't let me
If I go back I won't go back as me,
I won't be a familiar friend
I can't take any more losses cause I lost me loving you

I can't cry anymore
I can't do heart break that makes me feel like I want
to die.
I can't pray to god and ask him to bring you back
I can't feel like there's something wrong with me
anymore
It's over for that.
Your intentions became questionable
Once you made me question myself
I only want real around me
And now I don't know if I ever even
Had real around me.

No more looking back. I'm tired of looking back. I'm tired of going back and forth. I'm sorry we met when we did. I'm sorry it's not the time. I'm sorry that you can't see that you can do this life thing with me. We got this. Sorry you can't see that we go together. I just want to love you and build. But you've made room in your mind to think about whether you will find something better. You just look at me and think you're settling. As if I'm not the best thing that will ever happen to you. As if I don't love me enough to always be better. You made a bet on our bond and you lost it all. You sacrificed our love for like. You're out there looking for a fake version of us when you had the real on your entire tongue. My mind, body, and soul on your entire tongue. You tasted everything. Our kisses were sex in itself. You had me. You had me like no one else ever did and ever will.

I'm sorry I've always wanted what was best for my best friend. I always wanted to grow with you and I saw my dreams and my desires in the palms of your hands trailing along your veins. As I looked down at my left hand I always knew I wanted you to be the one. I was down for you... I loved you like you were my son. I still love you like you are my son. I got a mother's love for you. I know I heard you say you would die for me so many times, how you would do time for me if anyone ever tried to hurt me. You were the one hurting me. So lucky that I came across someone who said they would die for me, but couldn't even stand by my side. How does that work? .
I mean you'd be here and it was great. But now it's March and the seasons are changing and I have to deal with my love leaving again.

For the last time. I'm making this the last time.

Fallen.

From the looks of it, things are always too good to be
true
Always knew we would get here
Baring all arms fighting for love
The love we wished would have come later on
This young love we want when we're old
Because right now too much is going on
Here we are trying to make it last forever.
Not knowing any better.

How does the perfect love separate, how could ya'll
let me down?

Guess they were looking for the culprit.

Told them life happens. Life forced us to let go.
I mean looking back it all makes sense
But who wants to make sense when they just want to
make love

To the love of their life.

Numb.

I apologize to myself for making myself numb
For talking down on love
As if it's not the best thing I've ever felt
Whenever I came face to face with it
Whenever I was far and still felt it
I still wanted it,
I still felt the same.
I still wanted to sacrifice my youth,
My hoe days,
That are so embraced I guess I'm missing out
Cause here I am single and they can't tell the
difference
I'm still missing out
I've been watering this love thing down
Acting like I don't feel
Like I can't stand the thought of someone adoring me
Because I don't want just anyone gazing in my eyes
Falling in love with everything I do
Maybe I'm just numb with everyone
But you
I just want to apologize you know
Cause I've been lying to me
Actually crying deep inside
Under all the uncertainty and

To Showing Myself More Love,

Frustration wondering
Why is it so complicated for us

Why can't you sacrifice?
Nip it in the butt,
Face me.

We're perfect,
Look, face me
Allow me to give you everything you want
Cause I know love
I know I'm acting numb because
my love runs deep
All up and through me
I can find someone who knows my worth
I can find someone to calm my nerves
I can find a good time
That illusion of love that feels everlasting
In the moment
But after the moments
I'm still sitting here hoping
You're out there, somewhere,
Actually I hope you're everywhere
Being numb with
Everyone but me
Face to face

Still hoping.

53

It's happening again

I get anxiety every time I get close to someone new. Part of me still feels like I owe you. Even though I've given you so much of me. Even though I never asked for it back. I still feel like I owe you loyalty. Distance can never change that even when we've failed as lovers. I still feel like I owe you as a friend. *When does your best friend stop being your best friend?*

notes:

You don't get to put people on hold for when you're ready to love them because you're not ready now. That's not what meant to be is about. Meant to be is what already is. Being there, non-stop. It's about who you choose to love and them choosing you back. So the next time you decide to tell someone you're not ready but you see them for you in the future, make sure to tell them why you don't see them for you right now, and how they're actually just not the one for you right now. How you can't be completely honest with them because you care about their heart. But how if they moved on it would be okay. Like it would actually relieve your guilt because it would mean for you they wasn't really the one for you anyway. Something you already knew.

Keep Searching.

Sometimes you have to understand that they were
never in love with you.
they couldn't grasp your reality
They just loved that you loved them.
They loved what you did and how you did it.
They just cared about you. But they didn't see it with
you.
And that's ok.
It's ok if someone just cares about you. Let them care.
platonic love is still love.

Well I can't seem to understand what's what these days, sometimes it's 1am and when I pull my curtains back I expect the moon and then the sun comes through, now we both know that ain't right, but I don't want it to be wrong.

Losing.

She sits and wonders about her decisions [the
precision]
Her decisions and choices that never seem to work,
they never seem to fix the situation at hand
Like how to bring you near and keep you close
without you wandering off
like does she let him do him or does she do her while
he's in the midst of him doing him
is it okay for her to protect her own sanity by pushing
him away after he pushed her away thousands of
time, or is this tit for tat
so self-righteous of him to think her only entitlement
is to be on call whenever he needs her
she sat as she had been placed on hold, once again,
conforming to the doubts of another, your life is too
precious to be put on hold and for the I don't knows,
when there is someone out there who is so sure.
you ought to get to know yourself, I think it's time
you call yourself and spend some time with yourself
and get in tune with how special you are.

she sat and thought maybe if she took all the love that
she poured into him that he never thought to retain
you know all that love that spilled over because it just
wouldn't fit
maybe just maybe if she poured all that love into
herself, she'll be confident in any decision she decides
to make from here
she deserves to feel good and empowered to choose
herself and to not just be okay for *now*, lonely for
now, feeling loved for now, feeling as if she's the one
for *now*
she sat and felt like practice
while he's so sure, manipulation never destroyed him
so there she is unlearning what she thought love was,
she sat and thought about making changes to herself
physically, because mentally she couldn't beat him at
his game.
No haircut, no weight loss, no weight gain, no hips, or
dyed hair can make a man that's not for you see you
as the gem you are, he's not deserving of your
thoughts and wishes of him being the one
you deserve more than to second guess whether you
want to pick up the phone because you know it's no
good but it'll feel good for the night, you deserve to
wear your heart on your sleeve for the right one
you should be looked at as eye candy always in all
ways that are you, in ways that serve you while you
stay true to you

She sat and thought about how long it took for her to
act upon her worth, how she always knew who she
was but would sometimes get confused
that's what happens when you give too much of
yourself away without confidence being embedded In
the palm of your hands
testimonies

Some of our darkest days have never been spoken of,
we'll hold on to the days we've hurt, the days we've
damaged others, blaming ourselves blaming others,
defeating our joy, wondering why and how could this
be, why be a good person if this will happen to me?
We'll sabotage our growth, stuck in a place that feels
comfortable stuck in a place that caresses our hurt,
unforgiving, not living for today, but dying for the
days, the moments, that we wish we could rewind
back to, to do different, to be different. Days of
tearing yourself down based on fault. Why didn't I
know better then? Because everyone needs a
testimony. There's truth there, proof of your strength,
proof of awareness and of your acceptance in order
to open new doors. Doors that welcome
improvement and truth, doors that welcome the *new
you.*

healing.

To those who wish to love me,
Understand that I'm having a hard
Time trying to figure out your intentions with me.
I hear you want me
I hear you want to give us a try
But understand I've known many pretenders
I've seen things
I've heard stories that made me pray to God
"Don't ever let me go through that"
I couldn't fathom.
In this world where being yourself is not seen as cool
I don't want to fall for anyone who's everyone but
Who I thought they were.
Pretenders, liars,
Two things I despise
Please don't do anything you're going to have to lie
about.
Please don't pretend for me to stop from hurting me.
I've been hurt before
I don't mind being hurt again
I can't allow someone I don't know to tell me they
love me

Because 9 times out of 10 you don't know me
You have only tasted me
You have only felt my exterior.
You don't know my soul.
You have only felt my walls
Not as my man
But as a potential

You don't know how this love comes down
So you haven't even felt my greatness
You haven't felt how at home I can make you feel
The sun rises and sets here
The warmest thing you've ever felt
You don't know me

And I'm afraid that when you get to know me
Below the surface
You'll be too disappointed
Because I'm too deep for you
Or maybe too shallow
Because my love doesn't love for just anyone
Who says they want to love me
I don't care about what you have
Or what you can do for me
If you can't turn my mind on and
Set this volcano off in my stomach
That doesn't mind waiting to be set off
Don't front for me.
Be yourself for me.

I might love you.

Not Right Now.

Here you are ready to give me
Everything I never had that would make me smile
Here you are seeing the God-like woman in me
That one too many couldn't see
At a time where I just want to enjoy my god like self
Don't tell me you love me
I will only pause, smile, and say thank you
Please don't shake your head and call me a savage,
I'm still sweet
Trust me I did not say it in vain
It's just that it took me awhile to get here
And I like it here
I really do, I mean it's a different
High
This pedestal I had to walk many steps to get to
So yes, thank you
For telling me you love me
Cause that makes two of us
At least we agree on something

At least that's a start

Understand that I'm selfish these days
And I just need someone
Who won't judge me for it
I'm finally here in love with everything
That I am
I just want to get lost in my world
I mean no disrespect
But please don't ever feel like you're doing me a favor
By admiring me
Please don't ever talk to me like I need saving
I am saved
I'm perfectly fine and unavailable
To be everything you need
I've been everything to everyone
There's still some pieces of me that are still out there
That I want back and can't get back
So thank you,
I love me too,
Lord knows I just want to love me too and I really
want to give me
Everything just like you.

To Showing Myself More Love,

Thank you for letting me go,
God knows I wouldn't have chosen me
Over us
Thank you for choosing you for us.

Questions...

Did you get everything you wanted?

Did you find out if we were doing it wrong?

Do you fight the urge to speak to me every day?

Am I worth the sacrifice?

Have you still been thinking about me a lot lately?

Did you figure out that no one can love you the way I love you?

No one can make you feel at home how I made you feel at home.

Did you realize how it was always all about you?

How everything revolved around you... I made
everything fit for you. How the love we made could
never be topped because we were soulmates, we
branded our love through blessings from the higher
up and on picture frames that shouted forever we
knew it was a blessing at a point we still know that
it's a blessing, even through distance to have
someone who loves you enough to see you sprout
through miles, new lovers, new friends, street lights
apart, red light green light, 1,2, free, I let you free and
now you can't help but roam back to me.
When highway traffic stops you from getting close to
the one thing that made you believe in God's timing.
Until it came to an end and we no longer wanted to
believe God's timing because it no longer worked in
our favor. When all you want to do is reach me by
12:30 but you got there by 12:31 and I was already
gone and now you just want to scream because you

were so close to the affection that made the sun rise
inside of you.

Did you finally lose me? Kind of goes against
everything I once believed. When I believed it was us
that was meant to be. But what does meant to be
actually mean. Is it just for the moment and are some
moments longer than others? I thought I had it
figured out. Was our moment for years until we were
finally capable of letting go even though we still
loved. What does it mean when you can live without
someone, happily? Does it mean you were never in
love with them? Because I'm happy and I feel joy. Or
does it mean you love yourself enough to allow them
to grow and become all that they are? Like do I love
myself so much that it spills over into you and
everyone around me? Have I grown and glowed that
much? Have I blossomed that much enough to
understand the scrutiny?

understanding:

Some days I feel nothing, some days I feel everything.
Every day I know things are going to get better. Even
if I can't push myself to go out and do *life* that day.
Even if I'm feeling sorry for myself and regretting all
the decisions I ever made. When I'm sitting there
saying to myself "you should have left a long time
ago" or "it should have never got this deep" or "when
are you going to figure things out". But I remember
that I wasn't as strong as I am now. I thought being
strong was being able to cry and get through the
tears and go back. Never realizing I was settling. I
thought it meant riding out and putting others first.
Now I know that's not what being strong is all about.
It's about being able to stand on your own and
mentally knowing when it's time to stand on your
own and doing just that.

Being strong is being able to put yourself first and walking away from someone you love because they can't love you how you deserve to be loved. Walking away from your best friend who can't be the best lover. So even though I'm good and I'm living without them, I still feel resentment from time to time. I still feel like I deserve an apology. Part of me still wants them to come back and fight for me and pour out their love. I'm still healing, I still get mad at myself, I still want to place blame, and I still think about their safety. Sometimes I wish I never hurt them so all the bad can be placed on them. I'm being honest. Sometimes I still think I'll never form a bond like that again.

Part of me still wants that part of them that I can't get, but my mind says I'll never go back. So I appreciate when I feel everything, it lets me know that I'm human, and I've felt everything and I'm able to love deeply. And I would rather feel everything than to feel nothing at all. When I'm numb I'm not happy, I'm suppressing my feelings, I'm suppressing my wholeness and all the love that I'm capable of giving. I don't want to give my love to anyone but myself nowadays, I feel like I owe myself so much. I got a lot of making up to do with myself. I just need time off from anyone needing me or my energy. I'm still rejuvenating and trying to find my way. I don't want to bother anyone with the ups and downs of my healing process, so I keep them in arms reach not chest to chest, I don't want anyone kissing me on my forehead to remind me of how precious I am. I don't want to be hugged so tightly that the smell of their cologne makes me weak. I don't want to smile too big because I might make them feel as if they make me happy. I don't want to say anything that may signal

that I'm in it for the long run because tomorrow I'm
bound to wake up feeling different. That smile may

turn into a gaze of uncertainty. Uncertain of them,
me, where I want to be, the time, the timing, the
intentions, whether I'm ready or not, and if I'll ever
be ready again. So I just want to be free, I just want
everyone at arm's reach.

at arm's reach:

where you're a friend and don't mind being patient while I figure me out.. Where you study me in this process and watch me blossom from head to toe and not just at face view. Where you can see if you really want to take it or leave it. Where I can reach you when I'm ready to grab you and love you whole. Because you watched me heal and still want me in your arms.

letters:

I've been analyzing myself and figuring myself out.
I've been spending time trying to better myself and
my experiences. I may not know everything
pertaining to what I don't want and what I do want
but I am trying to figure that out everyday. I've made
mistakes that don't define me. I'm patient enough to
grow with myself and I now understand that no one
else is obligated to grow with me. I'm gaining more
confidence and accepting my individuality. I'm
realizing that I am unapologetic when it comes to
who I am as a person.

I no longer put the blame on myself nor do I put the blame on them for things coming to an end, for broken promises, for not being as loyal as me. Life is about living and learning. If I resent them I will continue to feel hurt within and my circumstances will not change. I cannot be focused on things that bring me pain because I cannot flourish if I am not watering myself with the tender, love, and care that I deserve. I can't fly with bricks placed on my wings.

Maybe you couldn't stay with me so many times because you were still finding out who you were. Maybe you weren't sure if I would be the right fit for the person you were becoming. The person you would want to attract wasn't me. Doesn't mean I didn't look good, or wasn't a good woman. I just wasn't enough for you. You just didn't want this good person. And that's okay. *I learned that everything is going to be okay.*

please don't ever settle, please don't ever beat yourself up for sticking around, please don't ever beat yourself up by sticking around.

enough, *the mantra.*

It's going to be okay because I am enough. I am enough for myself. I have enough care for myself to no longer hurt myself and to protect my heart. I have enough strength to walk away from something that meant everything to me. I have enough tenacity to cry one day, all day, let it all out and smile again the next. I have enough faith to know there will be better days and I am only getting better. I have enough passion to want to be a better me not for someone else but for me because I have the best love for myself. I have enough confidence to acknowledge that there are so many beautiful women in the world. I have enough knowledge to know that I am one of them. I have enough happiness to spread love to others and make good energy contagious. I have enough good in me to make others feel good. I have enough bad in me to make it through anything that challenges my strength. I have enough love in me to know I am more than enough.

I understand that people don't have to love me back and that will not phase me. I know the best is yet to come. I am enough and I already have the best love from up above and deep within to live my life graciously. I am here for me and me only, my purpose isn't to be enough for anyone but myself. And when someone comes around they're going to see that and love me for just being me. I won't have to try hard. I will only have to come as I am and that will be enough for them. I just hope that they are enough for me, just as you were.

79

you were more
than enough,
i just wasn't
ready to grasp
it all, just
wanted you to
be more than
enough for
yourself, we
had some
growing to do
as individuals,
but you were
always my best
friend.

To anyone who misses who they were,

That's not who you're meant to be. The best version of you is yet to come. Please understand how necessary it is for you to learn yourself through different circumstances. And learn that you're capable of breaking down and rebuilding with new found pieces. But fight every day to find that person and I guarantee you that you'll find someone better. Someone you'll love and protect more than ever.

To anyone who's looking for me,
You won't find me.

You'll recognize my smile, but it'll be bigger so you won't understand.

You'll recognize my eyes, but they'll be brighter so you'll be blinded.

You'll recognize my walk, but it'll be more confident so you'll be mesmerized.

You'll recognize my voice, but it'll be much smoother so you'll soak in my words.

You'll recognize my ass, but you'll know that you can't dare touch that.

The conversation will be different. You'll think you'll have me figured out. But I am not the same. I don't do things the same. I lost touch with who I was and have not looked for her since. I have enough sense to not be so transparent when people like you come looking for people like *her* again.

to those having a hard time loving themselves,

Biggest mistake to make is loving someone else
before falling in love with yourself. Putting the
pressure on someone to love you more than you love
yourself. Or even worse having someone love you and
you don't understand why they do. You don't
understand how special you are, how rare you are,
how much of a difference you make and can make if
you dug deep and showed yourself more love,
compare less, give yourself more credit.

You're here you're alive dealing with your reality and
trying to change it. Life is beautiful even when it's not
all good.

Establish yourself before you allow someone to
validate why you are beautiful. You are beautiful
because you know you're a work of art. You're
beautiful because you're comfortable in your skin
you're beautiful when you're not comfortable in your
skin. You're beautiful because you work on yourself
every day, you wish to be better every day. You wish
to break through barriers that no longer keep you
safe. Never forget that there's still beauty in the
process.

You're meant to be you, you're meant to learn you.

83

To My Sisters.

I pray for you every day,
I pray for your safety foremost, because you just
never know nowadays,
I mean with everything going on, and how our skin
doesn't make it any better
So I pray.
I pray that you smile today and an epiphany comes
through
To remind you of how great you are as you are
How much love you have around you and inside of
you
No matter what you think you've lost... again
Or who's lost you... again,
I'm still here.
And you're still beautiful.
I hope you know you're better than you think and I
know you probably think the opposite every now and
then.
I sit and think about you all,
And how I'm so lucky to be able to give you all my
heart,
How I'm able to go where I'm celebrated and not
tolerated

Even when I can't give my time all the time or
Even when we disagree and when I'm mad at the
decisions you make
I still love you, I'm still going to defend you
You make me mad, you make me happy
Understand how special you are to have sisters.
We can tell one another about ourselves and laugh
about ourselves
Because we're sisters.
Know that I have your back when you think you have
no one
We laugh, we cry, we done spilled our hearts out over
and over
And the days where we can't understand ourselves,
and we've had enough but we don't know what
enough is and we know we're smart
But keep making bad decisions
Just know I got you
I want to see you succeed, and I want to see you full
of joy, full of freedom
Smiling, understanding all the pain I've witnessed
I'll probably witness it again because this is life but
I'll always be here.
I can't wait to see us grow through it all
I want to see us love ourselves more
Lets promise to show how happy we are to see one
another like when we see our lovers and show them.
When you think of bonds, know that this one can't be
broken
Because no matter how far you go,

To Showing Myself More Love,

We're Sisters.

I Know You

I know what it feels like to be you, I know how it feels to wonder if someone loves you for you or what you can do. I know how it feels to have the weight of everyone's burdens on your shoulders and still find the time to find the space to lean on your own.
I think we're capable of healing I think we know when we're better off by ourselves but would rather save the world. I think we give and give and sit and wait for our lovers to tell us to stop.
Even after we've already decided we don't want to fight for love anymore, I think we overstep our boundaries and misinterpret what it means to love,
We give way more than we get, we make promises that we'd die to keep, like when we say we'll always be there.
I think when we say we want this thing forever we mean it with everything
We're deep. We hurt a lot and we're still willing to get hurt again, I think we're understanding or maybe there's a lack thereof, they expect us to know better when we've never known better.

We want to learn, we extend ourselves to learn a little
more about our lovers every day, we stick around
because after falling deep in love it takes us time to
climb out of it
We're amazing beings, we deserve to feel beautiful
every day we deserve to know our presence is
appreciated, we deserve someone who makes plans
with us, for us
We're special, how dare we ever settle for
uncertainty, or abuse, how dare we give and give
until we're left with nothing, not even the urge to feel
something new, not even the urge to learn ourselves,
or stick around for ourselves. We're strong though,
I know we sometimes wonder who has our back,
when most odds are against us, when they like the
idea of us being goddesses but not the reality of how
godly we are

You deserve more than to feel like you wasted your
time after loving and loving someone who loved you
sometimes, you deserve someone who admires you,
and still isn't afraid to set you free, whose fascinated
with your wholeness and your trying to be
whole-ness without wanting to control you

I know you, I know you may be scared to lose them to
someone prettier, someone more established,
someone who isn't as real as you I know you're
thinking you're the best thing for them
You deserve someone who knows that, let's not
spend more time investigating than we spend leaving,
than we spend treating ourselves how we wish to be
treated,
I know you feel like you got the shorter end of the
stick but sister,
As long as you have love within you will always win.

to: hurt me,

I'm finally okay with letting people go and loving them from a distance if that means I get to keep my sanity. If that means I no longer have to question where I stand in their life. I never want to question where I stand in someone's life ever again. I just want to know. No doubts, where I can look them in the eye and feel safe with them. I'm at a point in my life where I'm 100% comfortable with being me and moving on my own time at my own rate. *I have people around me who don't want me to be anyone else but me.* Things I was once ridiculed for I am praised for. I have people around me who appreciate what I bring to the table and the manner in which I bring it to the table. *And I appreciate them back for staying around because it feels good here.* It feels pleasant and safe even amongst the madness. Amongst the *non*-sense they have a friend who is always going to be a friend. I dodge manipulation, I dodge uncertainty, I dodge people who can't put their pride aside for me, people who make me fight for them when they never intended on raising a fist. *I dont go into the ring alone.* I dodge people who treat me like I'm replaceable, people who make it hard for me to love them and trust them. Care enough to reassure me of my importance to you. People who want to change me, and alter me to fit their vision. *I only wish to be me.*

To my dearest,

I love you,
I know I don't get around to telling you that often I
know that's not the relationship we've built, how
ironic we're a family full of young girls and women,
yet a family who doesn't display affection
but I love you for your strength, I love your
perseverance for your kids. But I always wondered if
you loved yourself enough to go hard for you.
For someone who hasn't been to many places I see
you judge the outside world so much, I see fear in
you, fear to really live. I used to see that part of you in
me and I always felt like it made me fall short. That
part I wasn't proud of, I've seen you settle yet still be
superwoman for everyone else
I never sat down with you and asked you what do you
see for you, I don't think I've ever made time to ask
you what were your dreams, and what were you so
afraid of.
I'd like to know, I'd like you to go hard for me if you
can't do it for yourself.

to showing myself more love,

It's just that. Just that simple but so hard. Showing myself more love. Love. Love feels right, it's from the inside out. And it shows. When you're loved you just glow. It has a glow about it. It feels like everything that's good for the soul. It puts you in good spirits. It allows people who love themselves to gravitate towards you. It inspires people to love themselves a little more. It's like music that makes you want to dance, that favorite part of your song that makes you sing louder and makes you want to try and hit that high note. Love will make sure you're taken care of, mentally, physically, spiritually. It's that thing that lifts you up and gives you just the push you need. Without a doubt, love just feels like a sunny day, clear skies, and no worries. Love feels like a vacation where you can be free from your reality back at home. Love is a home that you'll miss. Love is an escape. You have love in you and you have to show yourself what love is and what love feels like. You have to be consistent with yourself. How you want others to treat you, you have to give yourself those same expectations. There are no exceptions. You can't expect someone to love you when you don't love yourself. The love has to match, it has to fit like a glove, it has to go together.

What stops me from going back to places and people who didn't know the sacredness of my love?

Self-love.

S
t
i
l
l
.

Still going through the motions
Still not trusting God and what he has planned for me.
I wish I knew what he had planned for me.
Still not trusting myself and my ability to be
complacent,
Too feel great,
To be open to better things.
I'm still not open to loving someone. I still get anxiety
when I lay with someone who expects me to be in my
feelings.
I just haven't been in my feelings to feel I've been in
my feelings to heal. I don't want anyone to feel
disappointed when they realize there's more to me.
It's deeper than what you see, I'm deeper than what
you see. And deeper than what you perceive me to be.
I'm usually whatever I want to be whenever I want to
be it.
I have this argument with myself that I'm not ready
and I don't know when I'll ever be. I can't put a date
on it.

To Showing Myself More Love,

I'm running out of I don't knows and maybe's.
I know I have people waiting on me to choose them.
I don't know. Maybe I'm just meant to be by myself.
I have people ready to prove themselves to me and
how dedicated they can be.
I get anxiety.
I still don't think I'll ever love someone so deeply
again.
I might love them but I won't have that mother/ son
love for them, that undying love for them.
The love of staring at how beautiful they are when
they sleep, how you feel like part of them when you
hear their heartbeat while you lay your head on their
chest.
I feel like whatever feelings I feel will fade one day.
I don't want to hurt anyone.
I don't want to let anyone down.

I'm still trying to lift myself up and believe in myself.
I'm trying to find the confidence I need to remind
myself that I'm great.
I forget sometimes when I look back at past
disappointments.
I'm still trying to forgive myself.
Still trying to figure out what I could have done
differently if I could have been different.
Still wondering why I didn't know then what I know

now.
Maybe they would still be here. I'm still pushing
people away when they get too *close.*
Still looking for something to be wrong, for
something to go wrong when it's right.

Still wondering if what I deserve is what I want. Is it
still called settling when I choose someone who
treats me right even though I still want the one who
did me wrong.
It's a constant battle between choosing me and
choosing them.
I've been choosing me and questioning if it's worth it.
Did I lose out or am I the loss. Does it even matter?
Can I matter to me a little more?
I want to believe in me a little more and be better for
me, for my serenity, for my sake.
I'm still trying.

To Showing Myself More Love,

Do I ever want to go back?

Yes.

i still care, i probably won't ever stop, I'll always care deeply for those who've ever said *i love you,* for those who needed me to talk at one point, for those who needed me at 2am. but it's no longer up to me to fix people, to fix one-sided situations that are dying, it's no longer up to me to make feelings mutual. i've set myself free from those responsibilities.

Better Now.

I'm at peace with the fact that I'm putting myself first,
I changed for me and no one else. I changed to have a
peace of mind. I'm at peace knowing that I always did
my best, whatever that was at whatever time I
needed to be.
I'm better now.
Still learning, still wondering if I'm making the right
decisions. I still want to run away and hide
sometimes. I still wonder what if. I still love my old
love. I still find myself asking if I'm being too hard on
people when I set boundaries.
Still crying inside because well damn I still want what
I want. I still want to go back sometimes and visit the
past,
I still want that feeling back sometimes.
Sometimes I want to chance it to see if distance has
changed us for the better.
But I remember the only person I know for sure who
changed is me.
My mind is so gated now it stops my heart from
guiding my feet to places that no longer value my
presence. Places that no longer know who I am. I like

who I am. I like her enough to not allow her to be tolerated.
She's worth so much more. I'm getting to know her and she's getting to know me. I question my decisions

but not too much because I learned that I shouldn't have to.
Love is black and white. There are no grey areas.
Wanting someone in your life is black and white, you either care enough or you don't.
You pick, you choose, you gamble, you win or you lose.
I don't know if I'm winning or losing right now but I know that I'm choosing me, my happiness and my sanity even if it's for the moments.
I'm fine with just living in the moments.

the takeover.

*I don't even know who I am anymore but I like who I
see, I like how I feel. I like how I protect myself and stay
true to my values. I like that I prove things to myself
before I prove anything to anyone else. I feel proud, I
feel like no one can knock me off this pedestal. Even if I
slip, I trust myself to always regain my balance   to
have faith in my power. I've accepted that every day I
won't look pretty but every day I'll be beautiful.
Every day I'll be this work in progress while still being
a queen. I only let people around me who know that I
love myself. That's important to me. Don't ever look at
me like I need saving, look at me and wonder how I
saved myself. I saved all of this woman. I just want to
have people around me who look at me and feel free to
be who they are because I'm who I am. I am everything
I need to be at this very moment. This very moment is
going down in history with the other moments I
thought would be the death of me.
The other moments that became everything. Even
when I feel like I can be better. I don't have to explain
my heart to anyone, I don't have to explain my fight, or
what forced me to be silent and let go, I let God.*

*I let God speak for me and hopefully he got through to
you and anyone else who never heard me or let
misunderstandings stand for everything we've built.*

*I let my God, my higher power, fight my battles
because he's the only one who truly knows my heart
and my intentions, he knows I've tried my best, he
knows I never want to lose the race so now I just pass
the torch to him, I let God take over when I was done
fighting. I'm done fighting.*

101

Expired.

Old loves come back with old lines. That would have
had me once upon a time. I've learned that if they
were here, they wouldn't have to come back. I
learned to read between the lines of manipulation. I
only ask that if you dare come, come correct. Don't
come to see if you still have power over me. Don't
come seeing if you still have a chance while you're
still so very uncertain about me. Don't think for a
second that I'm the same girl I used to be, you will not
find the same person. I left part of her with you, the
other parts are somewhere around the city where I
dwelled and went for long walks thinking things
through trying to find the answers and shedding off
parts of you that I once adored.
Sometimes I wish I didn't have to be the way I am, but
when you protect your peace gracefully you don't
regret loving people from a distance, not when you've
fought for them at eye-view time and time again. Not
when you've said all you could have said. Not when
you didn't know what pride was when it came to love.

Gracefully I move forward, I push myself forward
even when I wish to stay still and hope that they
come back and catch up to me to love me how they
should have. I keep going. I know how I want to be
handled nowadays. I know I'm the reason people fell
in and out of my life time and time again was because
I let them.
I don't regret ever letting people find their way even
if it meant hurting me. But nowadays I've established
some boundaries. Boundaries that let people know
that I know about myself.
Boundaries that establish my worth. I don't want
nobody who makes bets with me, who says what's
meant to be will be, who doesn't understand that love
is love, but bonds are sacred privileges that need to
be cherished and not gambled with.
Bonds can be broken.
Handle them with ease.
For it is only memories that can't be erased.

I don't define my life based on people i've lost or let go but the love that was shared and the growth that came with it. I'll always love anyone I've loved because it helped me grow to be who I am. To love some parts of someone counts too, there's beauty in that too. That's why ex lovers are still distant friends because even if the relationship has changed through different phases of life the love will always be the same. This has always made it hard for me to figure out where I should be, being so forgiving and understanding, where do I truly belong?

mirrored love.

I just want to do *better*
I just want to do me and be better
be a better me for me, be good to me
is that a thing? treat myself, and feed myself, cuddle
me, become one with the one who has never been
number one, can I wake up and thank god for me, for
bringing me here, so far from home but never too far
to always find my center, out of my comfort zone but
comfortable in my skin, I owe me. I owe me some
time and some effort to keep on, keeping on.

I want to live my life so I can share my life.

*I had to find out what was important to me, find out
what made me happy, and what makes my heart smile.
I want to come across more things that give me
butterflies and I want to come across them more often.
I need more candles and RNB. I need more cake and ice
cream for my sweet tooth, I need to treat myself to
more things that make my feet swing in the air whilst I
lie on my belly. I need to borrow more no's and I can't
do it's because I'm doing nothing today, I'm not
fighting my sleep because I hate waking up drained.
I'm distancing myself from drama and the people who
bring it, I'm acting like I got shit to lose, I'm saying how
I feel when I feel it, I'm compromising with those who
compromise, but still compromising less. I'm doing
what feels good with who makes my soul feel good, I'm
protecting myself and acting like I know better, I'm
demanding respect by sticking to my values, I know I'm
valuable. I don't beat myself up for my mistakes I
apologize to myself and others, I let hurt go I welcome
love and understanding, I love from a distance too, I
tell myself "I'm proud of you" I tell myself "I'm beautiful
and strong and intelligent" I wake up and thank my
God for my life and my love because it belongs to me. I
wish I could full blown hug myself but in the meantime
I caress myself.*

107

Effortless.

As much as I wanted it I didn't want it. As much as I appreciated being held as if I needed saving. As much as I loved the random stroking of my hand and random kisses to my neck to let me know he yearned for me. Where I didn't have to chase and sweat the one I loved to get them to see I was glitter and gold; sassy and sweet; number one two and three. I just had to be present I just showed up every time as me, he felt the freeness the all I need is me-ness and still wanted to do the convincing that he could be of good use to me. All the time. Every time. He doesn't take for granted my smile, he makes sure he doesn't miss a beat, or the way I smirk and shy away at the sight of his camera to catch my random acts that he adores.

I couldn't understand why things were falling together at the time that it was falling together. But I knew it was falling together because of me. I was falling together. I was becoming whole the way I loved myself ricocheted off of all surfaces, all surfaces that were groomed and prepared to love someone who loved themselves. I attracted people who loved themselves, who wanted to love themselves, who were comfortable with who they were people who didn't need validation. I wasn't used to this.
I wanted to run away from something that was good to me, and go back to something I was used to. I had to stop.

I had to show myself more love.

When someone sweats you effortlessly. When all that matters is your here and now. That's the only love I want. Effortless affection. You just naturally want me and you just naturally *show me.* That's it. You crave me. My smell, my skin, its elasticity, my smile because it makes you smile. I appreciate the reminder that I'm beautiful even when I don't feel pretty. I appreciate that reminder that my presence is a present even when I don't feel like it'll make a difference.

You love parts of me that I just knew no one would dare caress.

moods/moments

As we lay you retain me in hopes that I'll stay. Arms
locked tightly around me for safety the transparency
of your energy makes it hard for me to question if
your energy is real. I knew big things would come
about after I'd stop asking you to be patient with me,
after I would give you the green light to pour
everything you've been holding back upon me. I've
fought off my anxiety for you, became more open to
the newness, erasing thoughts of you not being who
you say you are. I feel like you are who you are
because I am who I am unapologetically. How you
would unconsciously caress my hand in replacement
of wanting me all to yourself. You got me all to
yourself, every moment that you placed your hand on
my left thigh my right thigh shuddered with envy.
You feel good baby. Never thought I'd feel good
witcha. My nerves relaxed, my mind wondered if this
was it but my heart never questioned it. How come
you pull me in closer while we lay? As if you're scared
I'll go away, or is it to remind me that you're here *to
stay?*

" baby I ain't playing with you"

Conversations with God

Can I know why I can't quite put my finger on it? I feel like superwoman is finally getting a break from over-sacrificing to the undiscerning, he sees all the details of what I do of how I move, fell for how I groove. I tried to maneuver away every time I'd attempt to go awry you would tell me that it's actually okay. How come everything that was so tainted turned into things so sacred? Hate to think there's a time frame for it, hate to think I don't deserve it like I gotta be perfect. How can I feel I'm not ready when actually I'm intact and free? All in one piece all in one *peace*. How come I thought I would never find, another love for another that would grow inside of me? I don't know if I'm a new born baby or a queen with him. I feel like a *woman* who could dream big with him. You gave me a man who acts like he knows what this woman means to him.

To Showing Myself More Love,

I don't want anyone who won't fight for me or put their pride and ego aside. I fight and I put my pride aside. Reflect that same effort, that same love. Stop me from leaving, hate when I walk away. Pride aint got nothing on my passion when I'm passionate about who I love.

Worthy.

I have let go of anything that makes me question
myself.
I've let go of anything that makes me feel uneasy.
Anything that interferes with my growth.
Anything that picks at my confidence and doesn't
water it instead.
I've forgiven people who have no idea how much
they've hurt me or any idea of how much they've
altered my mind to almost not want to love.
Anyone who has no idea of the strength I had to find
to accept that I can't always get what I want, when I
wanted it badly.
When I've cried countless nights, unforgettable
breakdowns, praying I stop crying one day.
Now I want what God wants for me, I want it to
reveal itself over time as I reveal myself over time
and blossom into everything that has made me... me.
As patient and affectionate as I am with myself,
new love will reflect that and if it doesn't I still have
all the love I need.

I love myself harder every day.

115

To Showing Myself More Love,

Tough love is needed but so is the love that makes you believe in yourself more. Be gentle, protect yourself. Forgive yourself, and others. You are your most prized possession and even when you aren't happy with yourself and your decisions, understand that you're a work in progress. we all are. We're all trying to figure things out, trying to create a life that brings us peace and all the things we've dreamed of. Ask yourself for the patience you need from others when they handle you. Do your best everyday, some days that may mean crawling, for others that may be running sprints.

Show yourself more love.

Dear Self,
Share more of yourself. You haven't shared your
beautiful self with them, they don't know what you
love or what really makes your heart smile.
They don't know what you're crazy about but you
seem to know everything about them.
I used to think no one really cared about what I love
or what I was passionate about, I was afraid and still
am afraid of being too deep too quick. I'm afraid of
sharing who I am because of how people perceive me
to be. They might not like me anymore. But I like me,
I like me enough to share who I am with confidence.
What's for you is for you.
It's important to always be the you that you want
people to accept and love even if they do the
opposite. I didn't want to disappoint anyone. But I
was disappointing myself. I wasn't sharing myself
with the world. I was stuck on past bonds thinking I
would probably never bond with someone again.
How would I ever know if I always held back my part
of the bargain causing an imbalance, of me taking
parts of others and
pushing parts of me to the back
never giving them beautiful parts of myself
The world needs me, it needs me to ventilate, to air
out what I've been suffocating.

The feeling is different, you think you used to be
happy before based on who was in your life, until you
start loving on yourself and realize this is the
happiest you've ever been. This moment, where you
just want to say "Thank you God". But never forget to
thank yourself and pat yourself on the back. I only
want people around who are on the journey of loving
themselves, putting themselves first, learning
themselves, accepting and making themselves whole.
At a time where my focus has been myself. I haven't
done anything extra but pour love into myself and let
it overflow into everyone around me. I only had to be
me to be appreciated. I only had my love which was
appreciated.

Nowadays when I pray to my God the first thing I say is "thank you", sometimes I say "thank you so much" because I'm grateful for everything I have and everything I don't have. I know I already have everything I need to take me to the next step in my journey. I'm thankful to be able to see the good in everything, all things, being able to have an open mind and see through what may be hard to understand. I thank God for giving me the audacity to love again and again.

Wanted.

Trying to put the words together that could help make us stay together. Steady wondering who sent you and why and why me. knowing I deserve every bit of you, your good and your bad because I know you'll never be too bad for me. I've felt safe in your arms, I've fallen asleep on a chest curved just for the shape of the peripheral of my face, I feel at home with every hug. Every kiss lets me know I was missed. My movements have been studied and my mentality has been watched as if it holds a physical form, you're into me, nothing goes unnoticed i can't get nothing past you. , I never have to do anything that requires me to be someone else. You make me want to be a better version of myself. You've memorized my scent and appreciated my ability to keep it together.

But what about this....

What about this poetry. Is it sexy? Is it too deep for you? You know of me to be wise but what about this? What about my art? Does it scare you away is it of no interest? I know you told me you see everything and nothing goes unnoticed. Does me noticing everything, every detail, does me feeling everything so deep and making little nothings into somethings turn you off? can I turn you on with words that I've written during times where I've lied and said I was just chillin... just trying to put together words that could make us stay together. Scared to be every version of me because of how others perceived me to be, I am not her, I am she and me, I am this and that, I am both, I am everything I want to be, I only wish you see all of me and still want to come home, still holding me close, will you still take me for what I'm *worth.*

The other side...

deep down.

You loved me. You wanted me. Everything you said
was true from you not loving anyone else to you
being all for me.
I took for granted the small things thinking they are
small things not knowing how precious they were. I
didn't take my time to read between your lines, you
were poetry in itself but I wanted to read my book, all
the time... I read my pages day in and day out I didn't
think your book was worthwhile. I looked down on
your quiet nature and now I see how your silence is a
spark in itself, was I this blind? why couldn't I see
your energy, why couldn't I see how lucky I was to
have a love and friend who made me better. I wish I
could have been better for you.

You would have rode for me, you put me before you
and put me before you again... deep down I knew I
could borrow the world from you and you wouldn't
question when I'd return it
So much beauty in a woman who loves you more than
she loves herself without her knowing she isn't really
loving herself
I could have fell in love with you again if I believed in
you,
Had I had a bit more confidence in your being, had I
gave light and poured water on my grass I'd be
around to watch it grow.
I looked for new lawns
I took from you more than I gave, I acted as if your
light was dim as if you weren't anything serious as if
you were everything that could be replaced.
I didn't pay attention to your sacrifices, I paid
attention to your shortcomings
Now I don't see anything that you lack, you are
everything virtuous. Your heart your persistence to
love after you've been torn apart is intriguing, I'm
glued to the beauty of watching you love yourself
without having me to love,

you're worthy, you hurt me and you were still
worthy. Your soul loved my soul, I always wondered
why I came back and it's because you were home,

I didn't realize how big my home was, how
well-furnished and warm it was
The epitome of everything I want now,
I could have loved you better, I get it now, I pay
attention now, never noticed that freckle till now, or
how bright your smile is, how often you smile, how
often you listened, I'm having a hard time getting my
thoughts across nowadays, I've been more silent,
dying inside I miss my friend, I miss home.

i'll settle for friends.

Don't Fright

For life is about discovering, there's a life out there to discover, we have ourselves to uncover and to search for. there's courage in leaving behind those we love to pursue ourselves, there's beauty in looking back at moments and times that didn't make sense to understand the defeats that turned into lessons. i'll never want you to suffer from losing me, find your happiness, your cliche, find your God. I'll always be here, love will always be here, you'll always mean the most, look around at all the people i do not know, knowing you helped me find me, i can never not speak of you. I don't expect anyone to stay forever, but while they're here I'm only accepting love for as long as I can. Where there is a lot of hurt from letting go that means there was a lot of love. Through the hurt and resentment there is still a lot of love in the end. Love that says i want you to be happy and find what you want in life. Love that says i'll be okay with or without you. Love that says I'll still pray for you even though i can no longer lay with you. Love that understands healing and the motions. Love that knows no matter what they still have a friend.

To Showing Myself More Love,

Learn yourself and move on your own time, create a life that you love and then live it every day.

She doesn't know if she's truly in love with another because she's in love with herself. So she questions the depth of her feelings because they're not as deep as they once were. But that past dying depth and attachment streamed from the need for love from another being, streamed from the unknown of knowing any better, of not truly knowing love with no possession. Desperate times called for healthy measures. When you're whole, in love with you, you're already the one, who only appreciates the presence of number two.

1+1 =2.

127

To Showing Myself More Love,

*still on the road to showing
myself more love*

Thank you again,

I'm still not done, i still have so much more to say, so much more to experience, so much more love to give, so much more love to show. I hope this made you more comfortable with your journey. I hope you know its okay to not have it all figured out. I think it's important for us to do what feels good. Not just physically, but mentally as well. Do what feels good until you learn something about yourself. Protect your heart, your mind and your spirit. It's important to know that you matter and I hope this helps you matter to yourself a little more. I hope you've related to something here or at least gotten to know something about me as we become more acquainted. I hope we meet again as stronger people who are more aware of ourselves, people who love themselves a little bit more, people who give themselves a chance, and people who show themselves a little more love everyday. Or at least try to, there's beauty in the process too.

45345785R00080

Made in the USA
Middletown, DE
15 May 2019